In My Own Words

The Diary of
MARY JEMISON,
Captured by the Indians

edited by Connie and Peter Roop
illustrations and map by Laszlo Kubinyi

BENCHMARK BOOKS

MARSHALL CAVENDISH
NEW YORK

ACKNOWLEDGMENTS

The editors wish to thank June Namias, Ph.D., Charles Hayes, and Karl Kabelac of the Department of Rare Books and Special Collections at the Rush Rheese Library at the University of Rochester for sharing their expertise with us. Many thanks also to Pat Costello, Jo Kneer, and Laura Heller at North High School, as well as the staff at the Appleton Public Library

For our Canadian readers, and any others who use the metric system, here is a conversion table to help you with the measurements used in this book.

1 acre = 0.405 hectares
1 mile = 1.609 kilometers
1 square mile = 2.590 square kilometers

Benchmark Books
Marshall Cavendish Corporation
99 White Plains Road
Tarrytown, New York 10591-9001
Illustrations and maps copyright © 2001 by Marshall Cavendish Corp.
Copyright © 2001 by Connie and Peter Roop

Library of Congress Cataloging-in-Publication Data
Jemison, Mary, 1743-1833.
In my own words: the diary of Mary Jemison, captured by the Indians / edited by
Connie and Peter Roop
     p.   cm.— (in my own words)
Includes bibliographical references and index.
Summary: The experiences, based on her own account, of Mary Jemison who was captured by a Native American war party when she was twelve and subsequently adopted by the Seneca with whom she chose to remain the rest of her long life.
ISBN 0-7614-1010-4 (lib.bdg.)
1. Jemison, Mary, 1743-1833—Captivity—Juvenile literature. 2. Seneca Indians— History—Juvenile literature. 3. Indian captivities—Genesee River Valley (Pa. and N.Y.)— Juvenile literature. 4. Pioneers—Genesee River Valley (Pa. and N.Y.)—Biography— Juvenile literature. 5. Genesee River Valley (Pa. and N.Y.)—Biography—Juvenile literature. [1. Jemison, Mary, 1743-1833. 2. Pioneers. 3. Indian captivities—Genesee River Valley (Pa. and N.Y.) 4. Seneca Indians—History. 5. Indians of North America—New York (State)—History.] I. Roop, Connie. II. Roop, Peter. III. Title. IV. In my own words (Benchmark Books (Firm))
E99 .S3 J4564 2000   974.7004'9755—dc21   [B]   99-089750

Printed in China
3   5   6   4

To Edna and Morrie Brown of Rochester,
longtime family friends,
who inspired us to edit Mary's story

A STATUE IN MEMORY OF MARY JEMISON

Mary's Book

INTRODUCTION

Twelve-year-old Mary Jemison was caught in the war between England and France for control of the New World. The French and Indian War, as it was called, had been going on for years. France, with its stronghold in Canada, wished to possess the fertile Ohio River valley. England, its colonies running up and down the Atlantic coast, wanted to expand westward. The Native Americans—from the Iroquois to the Cherokee—whose lands these actually were, allied themselves at different times with each side.

Mary's family, immigrants from Ireland, had settled on a farm ten miles from present-day Gettysburg, Pennsylvania. Their farm was one of many scattered along the wilderness frontier. Between 1755 and 1758 Shawnee war parties, allies of the French, raided isolated farms like the Jemisons'. During these raids, cabins were burned, livestock was stolen, and settlers scalped and killed.

Frequently, however, white captives were taken alive and brought to the Indian villages. Some were tortured and put to death. Others became slaves. Many times, though, captives were adopted by native families in order to replace loved ones who had died. This was Mary Jemison's fate. She was adopted by a Seneca family to take the place of a dead brother.

After her adoption ceremony, Mary was no longer considered white, but a true Seneca. She lived with her new family, sharing the tasks that had to be done to provide food and shelter. Mary, who adapted to her life as a Seneca, frequently longed for her white family. But over the years, as she married and raised a Seneca family, she chose to remain with the Native Americans, even when offered the chance to return to the white world.

This is the story of Mary's capture and her life as a Native American. It is told in her own words as she spoke them at the end of her long and eventful life. Her words were set down by James E. Seaver, a local doctor, who did not want Mary's remarkable life to be forgotten. Mary's story is one of love and hate, of two cultures clashing, and of how a courageous woman, taken from one world, learned to live happily in another.

—Connie and Peter Roop
Appleton, Wisconsin

Selections from
A Narrative of the Life of
Mrs. Mary Jemison
Carefully taken from her own words,
November 29, 1823,
By Dr. James E. Seaver

My Family

Although I may have frequently heard the history of my ancestry, my recollection is too imperfect to enable me to trace it further back than to my father and mother.

It is my impression they were born and brought up in Ireland. My father's name was Thomas Jemison and my mother's, before her marriage with him, was Jane Erwin. I yet retain their mildness and perfect agreement in the government of their children, together with their mutual attention to our common education, manners, religious instruction, and wants.

They set sail for this country in the year 1742 or '43, bound for Philadelphia, in the colony of Pennsylvania.

The civil wars and religious rigidity and domination were the causes of their leaving their mother country to find a home in the American wilderness. Under the mild government of the descendants of William Penn, they might, without fear, worship God and perform their usual avocations.

avocations
(av-uh-KAY-shuns)
customary jobs or duties

In Europe my parents had two sons and one daughter: John, Thomas, and Betsey. In the course of their voyage, I was born.

They safely landed at Philadelphia. My father being fond of rural life, and having been bred to agricultural pursuits, soon left the city. He removed his family to the frontier settlements of Pennsylvania, to a tract of excellent land lying on Marsh Creek. At that place he cleared a large farm and for seven or eight years enjoyed the fruits of his industry. Peace attended their labors. They had nothing to alarm them save the midnight howl of the prowling wolf or the terrifying shriek of the ferocious panther.

During this period my mother had two sons, Matthew and Robert. Our mansion was a little paradise. Even at this remote period, the recollection of my pleasant home affects me powerfully, so that I am almost overwhelmed with grief. Frequently I dream of those happy days. But, alas, they are gone!

The Frontier

By 1700 the English colonies stretched up and down the Atlantic coast. As the area along the eastern seaboard was built up with cities and farms, colonists began to turn their sights westward. Gradually, they made their way across the Appalachian Mountains in search of fertile farmland. The frontier, when Mary was captured, was the ragged edge of the settlers' advance as they moved into the many river valleys draining into the Ohio. A storm was brewing, however, as the French claimed the Ohio River valley for themselves and resisted English movement into the region.

During the French and Indian War (1754–1763), the French encouraged the Indians to attack English settlers whenever and wherever they could find them. Many Indian tribes, including the Seneca, angered by the English having taken their lands, joined the French. The Seneca, one of the Five Nations of the Iroquois, raided isolated arms and settlements along the frontier.

Conflict

In the spring of 1752 and through the succeeding seasons, the stories of Indian barbarities inflicted upon whites frequently excited in my parents the most serious alarm for our safety.

The next year the storm gathered faster. Many murders were committed and captives were exposed to frightful deaths.

In 1754 an army to protect settlers and to drive back the French and Indians was raised and placed under the command of Colonel George Washington. But, after the surrender of Fort Necessity by Colonel Washington, the French and Indians grew more and more terrible.

The return of New Year's Day found us unmolested. Though we knew the enemy was at no great distance, my father concluded he would continue to occupy his land another season. The preceding autumn my father had moved us to either another part of his farm or to another neighborhood a short distance from our former abode. I well recollect moving, and that the barn was built of logs. The house was a good one.

I Am Captured

The winter of 1754–1755 was mild and the spring presented a pleasant seed time, and indicated a plenteous harvest. My father, with the assistance of his oldest sons, repaired his farm and was daily preparing the soil for the reception of the seed. His cattle and sheep were numerous, and according to the best idea of wealth that I can now form, he was wealthy.

But, alas, how transitory are all human affairs! How fleeting are riches! How brittle the invisible thread on which all earthly comforts are suspended! Peace, in a moment, can take immeasurable flight. In one fatal day our prospects were all blasted and death, by cruel hands, was inflicted upon almost the whole of the family.

On a pleasant day in the spring of 1755, when my father was sowing flaxseed and my brothers driving the teams, I was sent to a neighbor's house, a distance of perhaps a mile, to procure a horse and return with it the next morning.

I got home with the horse very early in the morning, where I found a man that lived in our neighborhood and his sister-in-law, who had three children. The man took the horse to go to his house after a bag of grain, and took his gun for the purpose of killing game. Our family, as usual, was busily employed about their common business.

Breakfast was not yet ready when we were alarmed by the discharge of a number of guns, which seemed to be near. Mother almost fainted at the report and everyone trembled with fear. On opening the door, we saw the man and horse lying, dead, near the house, having just been shot by Indians.

report
sound of gunshot

The Indians first secured my father and then rushed into the house and without the least resistance made prisoners of my mother, Robert, Matthew, Betsey, the woman and her three children, and myself.

My two brothers, Thomas and John, being at the barn, escaped and went to Virginia, where my grandfather Erwin then lived.

The party that took us consisted of six Indians

THE INDIANS RUSHED INTO THE HOUSE AND WITHOUT THE LEAST
RESISTANCE MADE PRISONERS OF US.

and four Frenchmen, who immediately commenced plundering. They took what they considered most valuable: principally, bread, flour, and meat. Having taken as much provision as they could carry, they set out with their prisoners in great haste.

Indian Provisions

When making war, the Seneca and other Indians carried little with them besides their weapons. They had to travel great distances by foot or on horseback and, if pursued, needed to move quickly. They hunted or fished as they needed food. Otherwise, they carried small cakes of light-weight pemmican, a mixture of dried meat, fat, and berries. When a raid on settlers was successful, the Indians took what they could easily carry: flour, meat, guns, knives, blankets, and kettles. Frequently they burned what they could not take with them.

On our march that day, an Indian went behind us with a whip, with which he frequently lashed the children to make them keep up. In this manner we traveled till dark without a mouthful of food or a drop of water, although we had not eaten since the night before. Whenever the little children cried for water, the Indians would make them drink urine or go thirsty. At night we encamped in the woods without fire and without shelter. We were watched with the greatest vigilance. Extremely fatigued, and very hungry, we were compelled to lie upon the ground supperless and without water.

At dawn we were started again on our march. About sunrise, we were halted, and the Indians gave us a full breakfast, using provisions they had brought from my father's house. Each of us, being very hungry, partook of this bounty, except Father, who was so much overcome with his situation.

Our repast being finished, we again resumed our march. Toward evening we arrived at the border of a dark and dismal swamp. Here we had some bread and meat for supper. The dreariness of our situation, together

repast
a meal

19

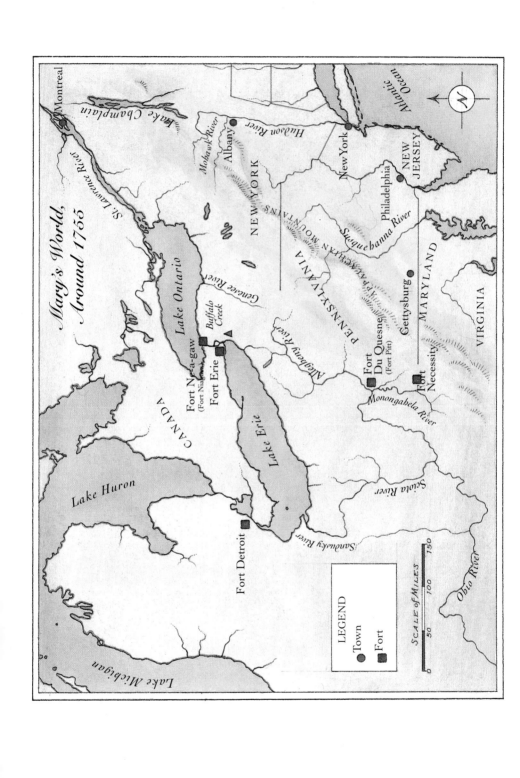

Mary's World,
Around 1755

Montreal

St. Lawrence River

Lake Champlain

Mohawk River

Albany

Hudson River

New York

NEW YORK

Atlantic Ocean

NEW JERSEY

Philadelphia

Susquehanna River

Genesee River

Fort Ne-a-gaw
(Fort Niagara)

Fort Erie

Buffalo
Creek

Lake Ontario

APPALACHIAN MOUNTAINS

PENNSYLVANIA

Gettysburg

MARYLAND

Allegheny River

Fort
Du Quesne
(Fort Pitt)

Fort
Necessity

VIRGINIA

Monongahela River

CANADA

Lake Erie

Scioto River

Lake Huron

Fort Detroit

Sandusky River

Lake Michigan

Ohio River

LEGEND

● Town

■ Fort

SCALE of MILES

0   50   100   750

N

with the uncertainty as to our future destiny, almost deprived us of the sense of hunger and destroyed our relish for food.

Mother, from the time we were taken, had manifested a great degree of fortitude and encouraged us to support our troubles without complaining. Her conversation seemed to make the distance and time shorter, and the way more smooth. But Father lost all his ambition in the beginning of our trouble and continued to be absorbed in melancholy.

Separation

As soon as I had finished my supper, an Indian took off my shoes and stockings and put a pair of moccasins on my feet. My mother, believing that they would spare my life, addressed me as near as I can remember in the following words:

"My dear little Mary, I fear that the time has arrived when we must be parted forever. Your life, my child, I think will be spared, but we shall probably be tomahawked here in this lonesome place by the Indians. O, how can I part with you, my darling? What will become of my sweet little Mary? O, how can I think of your being continued in captivity without a hope of your being rescued? . . . Alas, my dear! My heart bleeds at the thought of what awaits you. But if you leave us remember, my child, your own name and the name of your father and mother. Be careful and do not forget your English tongue. If you shall have the opportunity to get away from the Indians, don't try to escape, for if you do they will find and destroy you. Don't forget, my little daughter, the prayers that I have learned you. Say them often; be a good child, and God will bless you. May God bless you, my child, and make you comfortable and happy."

During this time, the Indians stripped the shoes and stockings from the little boy that belonged to the woman with us and put moccasins on his feet. I was crying. An Indian took us by the hand to lead us off from the company. My mother exclaimed, "Don't cry, Mary, don't cry, my child. God will bless you! Farewell! Farewell!"

The Indian led us some distance into the woods and there lay down with us to spend the night. The recollection of parting with my tender mother kept me awake, while the tears constantly flowed from my eyes. A number of times in the night the little boy earnestly begged of me to run away with him. Remembering the advice I had so lately received and knowing the dangers to which we should be exposed, in traveling without a path and without a guide, through a wilderness unknown to us, I told him that I would not go.

Prisoners

Early the next morning the Indians and Frenchmen that we left the night before came to us, but our friends were left behind.

It is impossible for anyone to form a correct idea of what my feelings were at the sight of those savages, whom I supposed had murdered my parents, brothers, sister, and friends, and left them in the swamp to be devoured by wild beasts! But what could I do? I felt a kind of horror, anxiety, and dread. I durst not cry! Durst not complain. My only relief was in silent stifled sobs.

My suspicions as to the fate of my parents proved to be true. Soon after I left them they were killed and scalped, together with Robert, Matthew, Betsey, and the woman and her two children.

Tomahawks and Scalps

Tomahawks were a favorite tool and weapon of the Indians, especially steel tomahawks. A tomahawk could be used to chop firewood, skin an animal, defend oneself, or attack an enemy. Tomahawks were decorated with beads, leather, porcupine quills, and even human scalps. History doesn't tell us whether it was white people or Indians who first began the cruel practice of scalping their enemies, but by the time of Mary's capture scalping was a common practice on both sides. Frequently, the scalping victim was dead when his or her hair, along with its skin, was cut off. Sometimes, however, the victim was alive. To be tomahawked meant to be killed by a tomahawk, usually by a blow to the head.

Having given the little boy and myself some bread and meat for breakfast, our captors led us on as fast as we could travel. One of them went behind and, with a long staff, picked up all the grass and weeds that we trailed down by going over them. By taking this precaution the Indians avoided detection, for each weed was so nicely placed in its natural position no one would have suspected we had passed that way.

After a hard day's march we encamped in a thicket, where the Indians made a shelter of boughs and then built a good fire to warm and dry our benumbed limbs and clothing, for it had rained some through the day. Here we were again fed.

When the Indians had finished their supper, they took from their baggage a number of scalps, preparing them by stretching them over small hoops and then drying and scraping them by the fire. They combed the hair in the neatest manner and then painted it and the edges of the scalps red. Those scalps I knew, by the color of the hair, must have been taken from our family. My mother's hair was red, and I could easily distinguish my father's and the children's hair. That sight was most appalling; yet, I was obliged to endure it without complaining.

In the course of the night, the Indians made me understand that they would not have killed the family if the whites had not pursued them.

The whole neighborhood, on hearing of our captivity, had turned out in pursuit of the enemy to deliver us if possible, but their efforts were unavailing. They found my father, his family, and companions stripped and mangled. From there, the march of the cruel monsters could not be traced in any direction. Our neighbors returned to their homes with melancholy tidings of our misfortunes.

The next morning we went on. At night we encamped on the ground in the open air, without a shelter or fire.

In the morning we again set out early and traveled, though the weather was extremely uncomfortable from the continual falling of rain and snow. At night the snow fell fast, and the Indians built a shelter of boughs, and a fire, where we rested tolerably dry through the night.

Before the fire was kindled, however, I was so much fatigued from running, and so far benumbed by the wet and cold, that I expected I must fail and die before I could get warm and comfortable. The fire, however, soon restored the circulation, and after I had taken my supper I felt so that I rested well through the night.

On account of the storm, we were two days at that place. On one of those days, a party consisting of six Indians, who had been to the frontier settlements, came to where we were and brought with them one prisoner, a young white man who was very tired and dejected.

In the afternoon the Indians killed a deer, which they dressed and then roasted whole, which made them a full meal. We were each allowed a share of their venison and some bread, so we made a good meal also.

Early the next morning the whole company, consisting of twelve Indians, four Frenchmen, the young man, the little boy, and myself, moved on at a moderate pace.

In the afternoon we came in sight of Fort Pitt, as it is now called. It was then occupied by the French and Indians and called Fort Du Quesne. The Indians combed the hair of the young man, the boy, and myself and then painted our faces and hair red, in the finest Indian style. We were conducted into the fort, where we received a little bread, and then were shut up and left to tarry alone through the night.

The anxiety of our minds drove sleep from our eyelids. It was with a dreadful hope and painful

WE WERE CONDUCTED INTO THE FORT.

impatience that we waited for the morning to determine our fate.

The morning at length arrived, and our masters came early and let us out of the house, giving the young man and boy to the French, who immediately took them away. I never learned their fate.

I was now left alone in the fort, deprived of my former companions, and of everything that was near or dear to me but life.

It was not long before I was in some measure relieved by the appearance of two pleasant-looking squaws of the Seneca tribe, who came and examined me attentively for a short time, and then went out. After a few minutes' absence, they returned with my former masters, who gave me to them to dispose of me as they pleased.

Soon the two squaws, along with my former Indian masters, were ready to leave the fort and sail down the Ohio River. The men set out first in a large canoe and the two squaws and myself followed in a small one. One Indian in the forward canoe carried the scalps of my family, strung on a pole that he held upon his shoulder. In this manner, with him standing in the stern of the canoe directly before us, we moved down the river.

At night we arrived at a small Seneca Indian town, situated at the mouth of a river called She-nan-jee. It was here that the two squaws to whom I belonged resided.

I Am Adopted

Having made fast to the shore, the squaws left
me in the canoe while they went to their wigwam
and returned with a suit of Indian clothing, all
new, and very clean and nice. My clothes, though
whole and good when I was taken, were now
torn in pieces, so that I was almost naked. They
first undressed me and threw my rags into the
river. Then they washed me clean and dressed me
in the new suit and then led me home and seated
me in the center of their wigwam.

I had been in that situation but a few minutes
before all the squaws in the town came to see me.
I was surrounded by them and they immediately
set up a most dismal howling, crying bitterly and
wringing their hands in all the agonies of grief for
a deceased relative.

Their tears flowed freely and they exhibited
all the signs of real mourning. At the commence-
ment of this scene, one of their number began, in

a voice somewhat between speaking and singing, to recite the following words:

"Oh, our brother! Alas! He is dead. He has gone. He will never return!

"Friendless he died, where his bones are yet unburied! . . . He fell in his prime, when his arm was needed to keep us from danger! . . . Oh, where is his spirit? No blanket nor food to nourish and warm him; nor candles to light him, nor weapons of war. Oh, none of these comforts had he!

"But well we remember his deeds! Though he fell on the field of the slain, with glory he fell, and his spirit went up to the land of his fathers in war! His spirit has seen our distress and sent us a helper whom with pleasure we greet. Deh-he-wa-mis has come. Let us receive her with joy! She is handsome and pleasant. Oh, she is our sister and gladly we welcome her here. In place of our brother she stands in our tribe. With care, we will guard her from trouble. May she be happy till her spirit shall leave us."

In the course of that ceremony, from mourning they became serene. Joy sparkled in their countenances and they seemed to rejoice over me as over a long lost child. I was made welcome amongst them as a sister to the two squaws. I

DEH-HE-WA-MIS HAS COME. LET US RECEIVE HER WITH JOY!

was called Deh-he-wa-mis, which signifies a pretty girl, a handsome girl, or a pleasant, good thing. That is the name I have ever since been called by the Indians.

It is a custom of the Indians, when one of their number is slain or taken prisoner in battle, to give to the nearest relative a prisoner if they take one. If not, they give him a scalp of an enemy. All prisoners that are taken in battle are given to bereaved families. Unless the mourners have just received the news of their bereavement, they generally save the prisoner.

It was my happy lot to be accepted for adoption. At the time of the cere-

happy
fortunate

mony, I was received by the two squaws. I was ever considered and treated by them as a real sister.

During my adoption I sat motionless, nearly terrified to death at the appearance and actions of the company, expecting every moment to feel their vengeance and suffer death on the spot. At the close of the ceremony the company retired, and my sisters went about employing every means for my consolation and comfort.

My New Life

Being settled and provided with a home, I was employed in nursing the children and doing light work about the house. Occasionally I was sent out with the Indian hunters to help them carry their game.

My situation was easy. I had no particular hardships to endure. But still, the recollection of my parents, my brothers and sister, my home, and my own captivity destroyed my happiness and made me constantly solitary, lonesome, and gloomy.

My sisters would not allow me to speak English in their hearing. Remembering the charge my dear mother gave me, I made a business of repeating my prayer, catechism, or something I had learned in order that I might not forget my own language.

My sisters were diligent in teaching me their language. I soon learned so that I could under-

IN THE FALL, THE CORN BEING HARVESTED, WE TOOK IT ON HORSES
AND IN CANOES AND PROCEEDED DOWNRIVER.

stand readily and speak fluently.

I was very fortunate, for they were kind, good-natured women, peaceable and mild in their dispositions, temperate and decent in their habits, and very tender and gentle toward me.

The town where we lived was pleasantly situated on the Ohio River. The land produced good corn. The woods furnished plenty of game, and the waters abounded with fish.

In the fall, the corn being harvested, we took it on horses and in canoes and proceeded downriver, occasionally stopping to hunt a few days, till we arrived at the mouth of Sciota River. Here we established winter quarters and continued hunting till spring in the adjacent wilderness. The forests were well stocked with elk, deer, and other large animals. The marshes contained large numbers of small animals such as beaver and muskrat, which made excellent hunting.

We all returned in the spring to the mouth of the river She-nan-jee, to the houses and fields we had left in the fall. There we again planted our corn, squashes, and beans, on the fields that we occupied the preceding year.

After planting time, our Indians all went up to Fort Pitt to trade with the white people. It was then that my heart bounded to be liberated. The white people were surprised to see me with the Indians, enduring the hardships of a savage life, and with so delicate a constitution as I appeared to possess. They asked me my name, where I was taken, and appeared very much interested on my behalf. My sisters became alarmed, believing I should be taken from them. They hurried me into their canoe and fled with me, without stopping, till they arrived at the river She-nan-jee.

Shortly after we had left the shore opposite the fort, the white people had come over to take me back, but after considerable inquiry and diligent search, they returned with heavy hearts.

Although I had been with the Indians for something over a year, and had become used to their mode of living and attached to my sisters, the sight of white people who could speak English inspired me with an unspeakable desire to go home with them. For a long time I brooded the thoughts of my miserable situation with almost as much sorrow and dejection as I had done those of my first sufferings. Then time, the destroyer of every affection, wore away my unpleasant feelings, and I became contented as before.

After visiting Fort Pitt, we sailed up the Ohio River to a place the Indians called Wiishto. Here we built a new town and planted corn. We lived three summers at Wiishto and spent each winter on the Sciota.

Marriage

That first summer in Wiishto, a party of Delaware Indians came up the river and lived in common with us. They brought five white prisoners with them, who made my situation more agreeable as they could all speak English.

Not long after the Delawares came to live with us, my sisters told me that I must go and live with one of them whose name was She-nin-jee. Not daring to disobey their commands, and with a great degree of reluctance, I went. She-nin-jee and I were married according to the Indian custom.

She-nin-jee was a noble man: large in stature, elegant in his appearance, generous in his conduct, courageous in war, a friend to peace, and a great lover of justice. He supported a degree of dignity far above his rank, and merited and received the confidence and friendship of all the tribes with whom he was acquainted.

Yet, She-nin-jee was an Indian. The idea of

spending my days with him at first seemed perfectly irreconcilable to my feelings. However, his good nature, generosity, tenderness, and friendship toward me soon gained my affection. Strange as it may seem, I loved him.

We lived happily together till the time of our final separation two or three years after our marriage.

Childbirth

In the second summer of my living at Wiishto, I had a child at the time the kernels of corn first appeared on the cob. It was a girl, but she lived only two days. It was a great grief to me to lose my child.

After the birth I was very sick. It wasn't until the time the corn was ripe that I was able to get about. I continued to gain my health and in the fall was able to go to our winter quarters on the Sciota River.

The fourth winter of my captivity, a son was born. I had a quick recovery and my child was healthy. I called my son Thomas Jemison to commemorate the name of my much lamented father.

In the spring, when Thomas was three or four moons old, we returned from Sciota to Wiishto. Soon after, we set out to go to Fort Pitt to dispose of our fur and skins taken in winter and to procure necessary articles for the family.

Indian Life

I had been with the Indians four summers and four winters. My desire to get away had almost subsided. With them was my home, my family was there, and I had many friends. They had treated me with affection and friendship from the time of my adoption.

Our labor was not severe and that of each year was similar. Indian women have all the fuel and bread to procure, and the cooking to perform. Their tasks are probably not harder than that of white women. Their cares certainly are not half as numerous nor as great. During the warmer months, we planted, tended, and harvested our corn, and generally had all our children with us. We had no ploughs but performed the whole process of planting and hoeing with a small tool that resembled a hoe with a very short handle.

Our cooking consisted of pounding our corn

into hominy grits and then boiling it, now and then making a cake of it and baking it in the ashes. We prepared our venison by boiling or roasting it. As our cooking and eating utensils consisted of a block and pestle [a tool for pounding], a small kettle, a knife or two, and a few vessels of bark or wood, it required little time to keep them in order for use.

In the season of hunting, it was our business, in addition to cooking, to bring home the game, dress it, and carefully preserve the eatable meat. We also prepared the skins, from which we made our deerskin clothes.

In that manner we lived, without any of the jealousies, quarrels, and revengeful battles between families and individuals that have been common in the Indian tribes since the introduction of ardent spirits amongst them.

spirits
alcoholic
drinks

The use of spirits, and the attempts to "civilize" and Christianize Indians by the white people, has constantly made them worse and worse. It has increased their vices and robbed them of many of their virtues.

The only thing that marred my happiness while I lived with the Senecas on the Ohio River

was the recollection that I had once had tender
parents, and a home that I loved.

My Leaving Wiishto

My Indian family had numerous relatives who
lived at a town called Gen-ish-au several hundred
miles away. Those of us who lived on the Ohio
had frequently received invitations from those at
Gen-ish-au to come and live with them. My two
sisters had left Wiishto for Gen-ish-au two years
earlier. Now a small group of us decided to leave
also.

Our party consisted of my husband, three of
my Indian brothers, my little son, and myself.
We embarked in a canoe that was large enough
to contain ourselves and our effects. As we left
Wiishto, it was impossible for me to suppress a
sigh of regret on parting with those who had
truly been my friends. I thought it doubtful we
should return.

We proceeded on our voyage up the river until
we arrived at a place called Yis-kah-wan-a
(meaning, in English, open mouth), where we
stopped. While there our party separated. I and
my son went on with my Indian brothers to

AT YIS-KAH-WAN-A, OUR PARTY SEPARATED. I AND MY SON WENT ON WITH
MY INDIAN BROTHERS.

Gen-ish-au while my husband went alone in the canoe back down the river. He decided to take some furs and skins that he had on hand and spend the winter hunting with his friends. He said that he would rejoin me the following spring.

My brothers and myself, with my little son on my back, set out for Gen-ish-au on foot. Only those who have traveled the distance of five or six hundred miles on foot can form an idea of the fatigue and sufferings that I endured on that journey. My clothing was thin and ill calculated to defend me from continually drenching rains. At night with nothing but my wet blanket to cover me, I had to sleep on the naked ground, generally without shelter. In addition, I had to carry my child, by now nine months old, every step of the journey on my back or in my arms and provide for his comfort and prevent his suffering. My brothers, though, were attentive, and at length we reached our destination in good health.

Gen-ish-au

Gen-ish-au at that time was a large Seneca town. We were kindly received by my Indian mother and the other members of the family.

My two sisters, whom I had not seen for so long, welcomed me with every expression of love and friendship. The warmth of their feelings, the kind reception, and continued favors that I received at their hands riveted my affection for them. I believe that I loved them as I should have loved my own sister had she lived, and had I been brought up with her.

No people can live more happily than the Indians did in times of peace. Their lives were a continual round of pleasures. Their wants were few and easily satisfied. Their cares were only for today.

Battle

At the time of our arrival at Gen-ish-au, the Indians were preparing to join the French to assist in retaking Fort Ne-a-gaw (as Fort Niagara was called in the Seneca language) from the British. They marched off the day after our arrival, painted for warfare and determined on death or victory.

Our Indians were absent but a few days and returned in triumph, bringing with them two white prisoners and a number of oxen.

The next day was set apart as a day of feasting and frolicking, at the expense of the lives of the two unfortunate prisoners.

One of my sisters was eager to attend the execution, but I felt a kind of horrid dread that made my heart revolt. On the morning of the execution she made her intention of going to the frolic, and taking me with her, known to our mother, who in the most feeling terms remonstrated against a step so unbecoming to the true dignity of our sex.

"How, my daughter," said she, addressing my sister, "can you even think of attending the feast and seeing the unspeakable torments that those poor unfortunate prisoners must inevitably suffer from the hands of our warriors? . . . And how can you think of conducting to that melancholy spot your poor sister Deh-he-wa-mis, who has so lately been a prisoner, who has lost her parents and brothers by the hands of the bloody warriors, and who has felt all the horrors of the loss of her freedom in lonesome captivity?"

This speech of our mother's had the desired effect. We stayed at home and attended to our domestic concerns. The prisoners, however, were executed by having their heads taken off, their bodies cut in pieces and shockingly mangled, and then burnt to ashes!

Life without She-nin-jee

I spent the winter comfortably. Spring at length appeared, but my husband, She-nin-jee, was yet away. Summer came on, yet he still had not found me. Then, one day, I received intelligence that soon after he had left me at Yis-kah-wan-a he had been taken sick. He died at Wiishto.

Bounty

In a year or two after this, the king of England offered a bounty to those who would bring in the prisoners who had been taken in the war. They were to be brought to some military post where they would be redeemed and set at liberty.

bounty reward of money

John Van Sice, a Dutchman, who had frequently been at our place, resolved to take me to Niagara, that I might receive my liberty and he the offered bounty.

redeemed bought back

49

I was notified of his intention, but as I was fully determined not to be redeemed, I carefully watched his movements to avoid falling into his hands. However, he saw me alone at work in a cornfield, and thinking he could secure me easily, ran toward me in great haste. I espied him and, knowing his errand, ran from him with all the speed I was mistress of, never once stopping till I reached Gardow.

He gave up the chase. But I, fearing he might be lying in wait for me, stayed three days and three nights in an old cabin at Gardow. Then I went back, trembling at every step for fear of being apprehended.

The chiefs in council having learned the cause of my elopement, gave orders that I should not be taken to any military post without my consent and that, as it was my choice to stay, I should live amongst them quietly and undisturbed.

elopement
escape;
disappearance

But, notwithstanding the will of the chiefs, it was but a few days before the old king of our tribe told one of my Indian brothers that I should be redeemed and that he would take me to Niagara himself.

In reply to the old king, my brother said that I

THE DUTCHMAN SAW ME ALONE AT WORK IN A CORNFIELD, AND THINKING
HE COULD SECURE ME EASILY, RAN TOWARD ME IN GREAT HASTE.

should not be given up. A serious quarrel ensued between them. My brother told him that sooner than I should be taken by force, he would kill me with his own hand!

Highly enraged, my brother went to my sister's house, where I resided but was out at that moment, and informed her of all that had passed respecting me. As soon as I came in, my sister told me what she had heard. Full of pity and anxious for my preservation, she directed me to take my child and go into some high weeds at no great distance from the house. My brother, she said, would return at evening and let her know the final conclusion of the matter. If I was to be killed, she said, she would bake a small cake and lay it at the door. When all was silent, I was to creep softly to the door. If the cake could not be found, I was to go in. But if the cake was there, I was to take my child and go as fast as I possibly could go to a large spring on Samp's Creek and there wait till I should hear from her.

Escape

Alarmed for my own safety, I instantly followed her advice and took my son and went into the weeds. Later, when I crept to the door, to my great distress, I found the little cake!

I knew my fate was fixed unless I could keep secreted till the storm was over. I crept back to the weeds, where my little Thomas lay, took him on my back and laid my course for the spring as fast as my legs could carry me. Thomas was nearly three years old, and very large and heavy. I got to the spring early in the morning, almost overcome with fatigue and at the same time fearing that I might be pursued and taken. I felt my life an almost insupportable burden.

That same morning, the old king came to our house in search of me to take me off. As I was not to be found, he gave up and went to Niagara with the prisoners he had already got into his possession.

As soon as the old king was out of the way, my sister told my brother where he could find me. He immediately set out for the spring and found me about noon.

The first sight of him made me tremble with the fear of death. But when he came near, so that I could discover his countenance, tears of joy flowed down my cheeks.

We both rejoiced, and after staying at the

I, DEH-HE-WA-MIS, WENT HOME JOYFULLY.

spring through the night, we set out together for home early in the morning.

When we got to a cornfield near town, my brother secreted me till he could go and ascertain how my case stood. Finding all peaceable, he returned to me. I, Deh-he-wa-mis, went home joyfully.

EPILOGUE

Through choice, Mary Jemison continued to live with the Seneca people for most of her life. She remarried when her son Thomas was three or four years old. With her new husband, Hi-o-ka-too, she had six children. They and their tribe lived quietly and peacefully until the outbreak of the Revolutionary War.

When peace came again, in 1783, the Senecas offered Mary the opportunity to return to white society with all of her children but Thomas. The tribe refused to allow Thomas to leave because they believed he would become a great warrior. Mary said, "The chief's refusing to let him go was one reason for resolving to stay. But another, more powerful reason was that I had a large family of Indian children to take with me. If I should find my relatives, they would despise them, if not myself, and treat us as enemies or, at least, with a degree of cold indifference which I thought I could not endure. . . .

"I told my brothers that it was my choice to stay and spend the remainder of my days with my Indian friends and live with my family as I had done."

Following this decision, the Senecas deeded Mary 18,000 acres of land, known as Gardow Flats.

Mary raised four girls and three boys. She gave all her children names from her white family: Thomas, John, Jesse, Nancy, Betsey, Polly, and Jane. Unfortunately, all three of her sons met with early, violent deaths. Nancy, too, died before her mother.

In 1823, when Mary was an old woman, she said, "I have been the mother of eight children — three of whom are now living — and I have thirty-nine grandchildren and fourteen great-grandchildren, all living in the neighborhood of the Genesee River and at Buffalo."

In 1825, the Senecas sold their land on the Genesee River and moved to the Buffalo Creek reservation. By that time, Mary had sold all but two square miles of her property. On these she lived with her daughters and their families. As Mary explained then, "Thus situated in the midst of my children, I expect I shall soon leave the world and make room for the rising generation."

However, in 1831, lonely for her Seneca friends and surrounded by white settlers, she sold her land and purchased a farm on the Buffalo Creek reservation. It was there in 1833, at about ninety-one years old, that Mary Jemison died. She is buried at Letchworth Park on the Genesee River.

EDITORS' NOTE

In 1823, Mary Jemison told the story of her life to
Dr. James E. Seaver. For three days, this petite,
blue-eyed woman about 80 years old recounted her
many adventures, from her capture to her final
decision to live with the Senecas. Mary's story of
sorrow and happiness mirrors in many ways the
conflict that was occurring between European and
native cultures.

Unfortunately, no copy of Seaver's original notes
remains to give modern readers specific information
about how he interviewed or transcribed Mary's story.
We do not know if he changed the order of her
account or the words she used, or if he deleted any
parts of her story.

We read various editions of Seaver's *A Narrative of
the Life of Mrs. Mary Jemison*, Canadaigua, New York,
1824, before editing the 1982 edition of his book. To
assist young readers, we modernized the spelling and
punctuation as well as organized and edited the
material for clarity. We relied upon the work of histo-
rians Rev. Charles Delamater Vail and June Namias
for assistance, especially with modern place-names
and some dates.

GLOSSARY

ancestry   family members from the past

anxiety   painful uneasiness of mind

avocation (av-uh-KAY-shun)   a person's customary
  jobs or duties

benumbed   numb, without feeling

bereaved   grieving for the death of a loved one

boughs   tree branches

bounty   generosity, goodness; a reward of money

catechism   religious instructions

constitution   the physical makeup of a person

countenance   a person's face and expression

dejected   disheartened, in low spirits

disposition   temper, personality

dressed   butchered

elopement   escape; disappearance

ensued   followed; began

fortitude   strength

happy   fortunate

hominy grits   corn kernels that have been hulled
  and coarsely ground

irreconcilable   opposed; opposite to

irreparable (ih-RE-prah-ble)   not able to be repaired

melancholy   great sadness

mode of living way of life

plundering stealing

procure get, obtain

redeemed brought back

repast a meal

report sound of gunshot

riveted firmly established

sowing (SO-ing) planting seeds, usually by scattering them

squaw an American Indian woman

spirits alcoholic drinks

temperate moderate

transitory changeable, temporary

unavailing unsuccessful

venison deer meat

vigilance with great care

TO LEARN MORE ABOUT MARY JEMISON AND THE NATIVE AMERICANS

BOOKS

Nonfiction

Doherty, Craig A., and Katherine M. Doherty. *The Iroquois*. New York: Franklin Watts, 1993.

Duvall, Jill. *The Seneca: A New True Book*. Chicago: Children's Press, 1991.

Griffin-Pierce, Trudy. *The Encyclopedia of Native America*. New York: Viking, 1995.

Graymont, Barbara. *The Iroquois: Indians of North America*. New York: Chelsea House, 1988.

Hakim, Joy. *The First Americans*. New York: Oxford University Press, 1993.

Murdoch, David Hamilton. *North American Indian*. Eyewitness Books. New York: Knopf, 1995.

Fiction

Durrant, Lynda. *The Beaded Moccasins: The Story of Mary Campbell*. New York: Clarion Books, 1998.

Keehn, Sally M. *I Am Regina*. New York: Philomel Books, 1991.

Richter, Conrad. *The Light in the Forest*. New York: Random House, 1953.

Taylor, C. J. *Little Water and the Gift of the Animals: A Seneca Legend*. Plattsburg, NY: Tundra Books, 1992.

CD-ROMS:

500 Nations: Stories of the North American Indians Experience. CD-Rom. Microsoft Corporation, 1995.

WEBSITES:*

Ohio Indian Heritage
http://www.ohiokids.org/ohc/history/h_indian/index.cfm

PLACES TO VISIT:

Letchworth State Park, on the Genesee River, about 35 miles south of Rochester, New York.
http://www.rit.edu/~ser9972/letchworth/letchworth.html

*Websites change from time to time. For additional on-line information, check with the media specialist at your local library.

INDEX

Page numbers for illustrations are in boldface.